T0380494

DR. ROBERT L. AKIKTA & DR. ROBERT LEE HARRIS

CRITICAL THINKING THROUGH ART

UNIT I

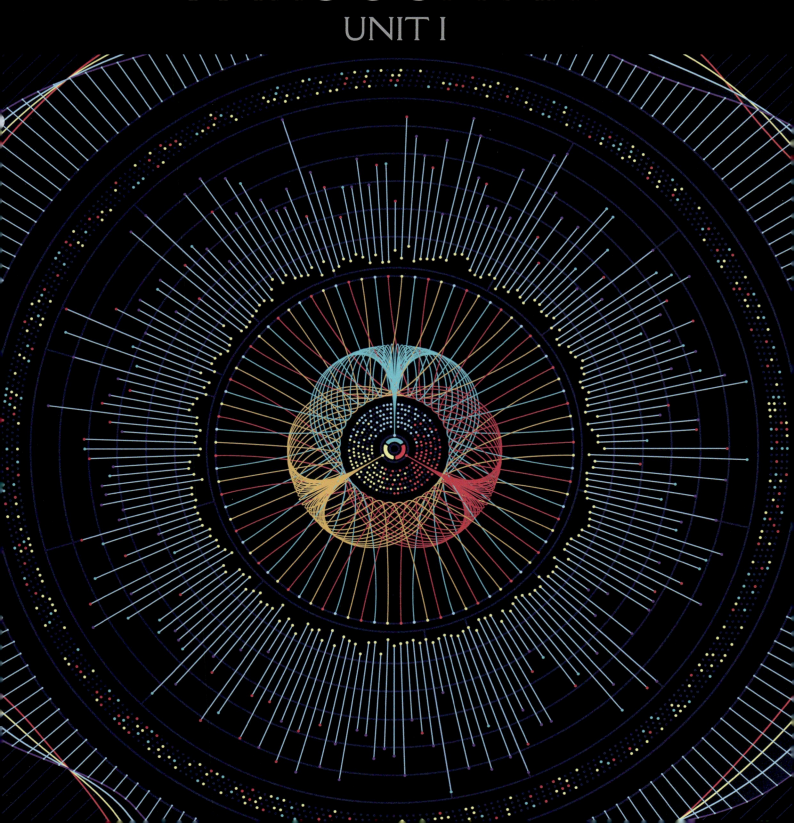

To order additional copies of this book, contact:
Xlibris
1-888-795-4274
www.Xlibris.com
Orders@Xlibris.com

CRITICAL THINKING THROUGH ART

UNIT I

DR. ROBERT L. AKIKTA & DR. ROBERT LEE HARRIS

About the Book

CRITICAL THINKING THROUGH ART UNIT I

This is an artistic workbook to empower the artist within you through critical thinking. This book will help you develop and explore many options that will overcome the restraints that block creativity. Our motto is: "Not even the sky is the limit." Trying this philosophy will directly assist the artist within you. You will find new options, new choices, and new energy to overcome limits and boundaries.

Working through the workbook's exercises and discussions will reveal new ways of seeing art, artists, and yourself. You will find that sometimes the artist has to dig a little deeper. You may have to face your biases and your old ways of creating art. Taking this step brings you into a world that overcomes methods that are tailored to your bias and old ways.

We will show you how you can be the artist that governs your art. You are the artist that decides the colors of the sky, the shapes of the mountains, the sizes of the waves, and the forms of life that most interest you. Together, with this book, a powerful and beautiful artist will be honored.

Thank You

Thank you for taking an interest in Critical Thinking through Art. This workbook was developed over the course of 30 years to help all walks of life in the area of ART. This simplified workbook is to help those who is starting out in ART. All ART is interrelated. Critical Thinking through an Art core concept is based on self-expression, which include:

- Life enrichment problem solving
- Critical Thinking
- Decision- making skills (Choices)

These concepts are provided to youth and adults regardless of what they know about art. Critical Thinking through Art also teachers core principles which will help youth and adults to reach their goal with their higher success rate by following these basic core principles:

- Stay focused by giving eye contact to whom or what is in front of you…
- Be still fully in what you need to understand that is being instructed…
- Be quiet and ready to receive useable knowledge …
- Ask prudent questions about what you don't know or understand…

Critical Thinking through art teaches all youth, adults and families: "Not even the Sky has LIMITS…"!

Dedication

We dedicate this book to Yahweh the Creator. It is our hope that those who use this book will grow in their understanding of the absolute mystery, to love and to dream.

To Amy, who is always supportive and truly behind me. She always encourage personal and professional growth while allowing me to pursue and share my passion among educators, the community and families.

To my mentor, Grandmaster Johnny L. Jelks, who always encourages me to do my best and to prioritize relevant principles in life.

These people have allowed me to prioritize my life and my deep spiritual relationship with God. I am blessed to have had them in my life. They helped me to grow as an individual and to perfect my knowledge and understand the meaning of words and how the two can move as ONE.

"Bright Idea"

"…Your "ID" is the stamp of your ideas… Which in-turns makes your ideas SHINE…"

Questions & Answers:

1. How <u>do</u> you <u>see</u> the picture?
2. Do you <u>like</u> the picture?
3. Did you <u>care</u> about the picture?
4. What <u>colors</u> do you see?

Class Discussion:

- Talk about the answers above.
- Side Note: There's NO Right or Wrong Answers.
- Give life/personal examples.

Class Project:

Create your own project.
- Suggestions:
    A. Draw your own conclusions of your version of the picture.
    B. Create a unique cotton clouds.
    C. Create different color schemes by using paints, clay, earth substance for different textures.

Summary/Discussion:

1. Take away
2. What you learned?

"Chillin"

"… There's nothing wrong to move from one play without using effort…"

Questions & Answers:

1. How <u>do</u> you <u>see</u> the picture?
2. Do you <u>like</u> the picture?
3. Did you <u>care</u> about the picture?
4. What <u>colors</u> do you see?

Class Discussion:

- Talk about the answers above. (Teachable moment)
- Side Note: There's NO Right or Wrong Answers.
- Give life/personal examples.

Class Project:

Create your own project.
- Suggestions:
    A. Draw your own conclusions of your version of the picture.
    B. Create a unique "Sleeping Device(s)"; Bed, Hammock, Sleeping Bag, etc.
    C. Create a Play, Clock, Timer, Chimes, Nature with soft musical instruments, etc.

Summary/Discussion:

1. Take away   2. What you learned?

"Good Morning"

"…There's nothing to "Morn" about when you can see the "Joy" that comes from the morning rays…"

Questions & Answers:

1. How <u>do</u> you <u>see</u> the picture?
2. Do you <u>like</u> the picture?
3. Did you <u>care</u> about the picture?
4. What <u>colors</u> do you see?

Class Discussion:

- Talk about the answers above. (Teachable moment)
- Side Note: There's NO Right or Wrong Answers.
- Give life/personal examples.

Class Project:

Create your own project.
- Suggestions:
    A. Draw your own conclusions of your version of the picture.
    B. Create a unique song or chant.
    C. Create a music sheets, puppets, chimes, etc.

Summary/Discussion:

1. Take away   2. What you learned?

"Me & My Shadow"

"…One can never understand other… If you can't understand who's within YOU…"

Questions & Answers:

1. How <u>do</u> you <u>see</u> the picture?
2. Do you <u>like</u> the picture?
3. Did you <u>care</u> about the picture?
4. What <u>color's</u> do you see?

Class Discussion:

- Talk about the answers above. (Teachable moment)
- Side Note: There's NO Right or Wrong Answers.
- Give life/personal examples.

Class Project:

Create your own project.
- Suggestions:
    A. Draw your own conclusions of your version of the picture.
    B. Create a unique "Cut Outs" by using paper, mirrors, photo's, etc.
    C. Create a collage, play, game boards, etc.

Summary/Discussion:

1. Take away   2. What you learned?

"Never Aim Low"

"… Never think for one second that your "Spirit" can't fly higher than the air beneath YOUR wings…"

Questions & Answers:

1. How <u>do</u> you <u>see</u> the picture?
2. Do you <u>like</u> the picture?
3. Did you <u>care</u> about the picture?
4. What <u>colors</u> do you see?

Class Discussion:

- Talk about the answers above. (Teachable moment)
- Side Note: There's NO Right or Wrong Answers.
- Give life/personal examples.

Class Project:

Create your own project.
- Suggestions:
    A. Draw your own conclusions of your version of the picture.
    B. Create a unique puzzle, kites, sailboats, etc.
    C. Create sounds of wind, air, motion, etc.

Summary/Discussion:

1. Take away   2. What you learned?

"New Day"

"… It's only a new day… If your NOT staying the SAME…"

Questions & Answers:

1. How <u>do</u> you <u>see</u> the picture?
2. Do you <u>like</u> the picture?
3. Did you <u>care</u> about the picture?
4. What <u>colors</u> do you see?

Class Discussion:

- Talk about the answers above. (Teachable moment)
- Side Note: There's NO Right or Wrong Answers.
- Give life/personal examples.

Class Project:

Create your own project.
- Suggestions:
    A. Draw your own conclusions of your version of the picture.
    B. Create a unique "Journal Book", "Diary", Take Pictures, etc.
    C. Create a "Time Line", "Time Capsule", Video, etc.

Summary/Discussion:

1. Take away   2. What you learned?

"Rainbow"

"... A "True" rainbow regarding the life of ALL people... ALL PEOPLE of difference..."

Questions & Answers:

1. How <u>do</u> you <u>see</u> the picture?
2. Do you <u>like</u> the picture?
3. Did you <u>care</u> about the picture?
4. What <u>colors</u> do you see?

Class Discussion:

- Talk about the answers above. (Teachable moment)
- Side Note: There's NO Right or Wrong Answers.
- Give life/personal examples.

Class Project:

Create your own project.
- Suggestions:
  - A. Draw your own conclusions of your version of the picture.
  - B. Create a unique clay forms of a rainbow, Water Art, Light Art, etc.
  - C. Create a Light/Water Show, Quilts Art, T-shirts Art, Pants, Socks Art, etc.

Summary/Discussion:

1. Take away   2. What you learned?

"Small Things DO Count"

"… It's not the effect of the many… It's the ONE that SUSTAINS…"

Questions & Answers:

1. How <u>do</u> you <u>see</u> the picture?
2. Do you <u>like</u> the picture?
3. Did you <u>care</u> about the picture?
4. What <u>colors</u> do you see?

Class Discussion:

- Talk about the answers above. (Teachable moment)
- Side Note: There's NO Right or Wrong Answers.
- Give life/personal examples.

Class Project:

Create your own project.
- Suggestions:
    A. Draw your own conclusions of your version of the picture.
    B. Create a unique "Object Art" (Small Pebbles Rocks, Coins), etc.
    C. Create a Rock Collages, Tier Art (Boxes, Picture Frames, Sea Shells, etc.

Summary/Discussion:

1. Take away   2. What you learned?

"Something to Think About"

"… It's the JOURNEY that keep you INTRIGUED… Not the END of the road…"

Questions & Answers:

1. How <u>do</u> you <u>see</u> the picture?
2. Do you <u>like</u> the picture?
3. Did you <u>care</u> about the picture?
4. What <u>colors</u> do you see?

Class Discussion:

- Talk about the answers above. (Teachable moment)
- Side Note: There's NO Right or Wrong Answers.
- Give life/personal examples.

Class Project:

Create your own project.
- Suggestions:
    A. Draw your own conclusions of your version of the picture.
    B. Create a unique puzzle(s), short Story(s), poem(s), etc.
    C. Create a documentary, short film, info commercial, commercial, needlepoint, graffiti, etc.

Summary/Discussion:

1. Take away   2. What you learned?

"EVERYONE HAS THE POWER FOR GREATNESS, NOT FOR FAME BUT GREATNESS, BECAUSE GREATNESS IS DETERMINED BY SERVICE."

- Dr. Martin Luther King Jr.

Questions & Answers:

1. How <u>do</u> you <u>see</u> the picture?
2. Do you <u>like</u> the picture?
3. Did you <u>care</u> about the picture?
4. What colors do you see?

Class Discussion:

- Talk about the answers above.
- Side Note: There's NO Right or Wrong Answers.
- Give life/personal examples.

Class Project:

Create your own project.
- Suggestions:
    A. Draw your own political cartoon making your commentary on life.
    B. Create a journal or pictorial diary.
    C. Create a color scheme by using paint or cut and paste colored paper or create a sculptural piece out of clay, plaster, Papier-mâché, or cardboard.

Summary/Discussion:

1. Take away
2. What you learned?

"IF I AM NOT FOR MYSELF, WHO WILL BE FOR ME? IF I AM ONLY FOR MYSELF, WHO AM I? IF NOT NOW, WHEN?"
-Rabbi Hillel

Questions & Answers:

1. How <u>do</u> you <u>see</u> the picture?
2. Do you <u>like</u> the picture?
3. Did you <u>care</u> about the picture?
4. What <u>colors</u> do you see?

Class Discussion:

- Talk about the answers above.
- Side Note: There's NO Right or Wrong Answers.
- Give life/personal examples.

Class Project:

Create your own project.
- Suggestions:
    - A. Draw sculpt, journal or create your own interpretation or your version of the picture and quote.
    - B. Create a unique "Self-Mirror"
    - C. Create your own photos, drawings, poems or scrapbook of emotions.

Summary/Discussion:

1. Take away
2. What you learned?

"PRESTIDIGITATION – Don't believe everything that you <u>HEAR</u> and only half of what you <u>SEE</u>."

Questions & Answers:

1. How <u>do</u> you <u>see</u> the picture?
2. Do you <u>like</u> the picture?
3. Did you <u>care</u> about the picture?
4. What <u>colors</u> do you see?

Class Discussion:

- Talk about the answers above.
- Side Note: There's NO Right or Wrong Answers.
- Give life/personal examples.

Class Project:

Create your own project.
- Suggestions:
    A. Draw your own conclusions about the meanings of the picture.
    B. Create a unique cotton ball or yarn interpretation.
    C. Create different color schemes using crayons, colored pencils etc. Use earth substances for different textures. Maybe try and sculpt it.

Summary/Discussion:

1. Take away
2. What you learned?

MOTHER AND SON

Questions & Answers:

1. How <u>do</u> you <u>see</u> the picture?
2. Do you <u>like</u> the picture?
3. Did you <u>care</u> about the picture?
4. What <u>colors</u> do you see?

Class Discussion:

- Talk about the answers above.
- Side Note: There's NO Right or Wrong Answers.
- Give life/personal examples.

Class Project:

Create your own project.
- Suggestions:
    A. Draw and or paint your own interpretations of what is happening in the picture.
    B. Create a unique cut and paste painting.
    C. Create in your journal a collection of poems and thoughts about this image.

Summary/Discussion:

1. Take away
2. What you learned?

PICK 'N COTTON

Questions & Answers:

1. How <u>do</u> you <u>see</u> the picture?
2. Do you <u>like</u> the picture?
3. Did you <u>care</u> about the picture?
4. What <u>colors</u> do you see?

Class Discussion:

- Talk about the answers above.
- Side Note: There's NO Right or Wrong Answers.
- Give life/personal examples.

Class Project:

Create your own project.
- Suggestions:
    A. Recreate your own version of the picture.
    B. Create an unique cotton ball and construction paper mosaic.
    C. Create different color schemes by using paints and other substances to create different textures.

Summary/Discussion:

1. Take away   2. What you learned?

THE CLOWNS

Questions & Answers:

1. How <u>do</u> you <u>see</u> the picture?
2. Do you <u>like</u> the picture?
3. Did you <u>care</u> about the picture?
4. What <u>colors</u> do you see?

Class Discussion:

- Talk about the answers above.
- Side Note: There's NO Right or Wrong Answers.
- Give life/personal examples.

Class Project:

Create your own project.
- Suggestions:
    A. Paint your own version of the picture.
    B. Create your own self-portrait by using paints, clay, wood 3-D printer etc. Take a photo cut it out, rearrange it and paste it back down making it into a collage.

Summary/Discussion:

1. Take away   2. What you learned?

Dr. Robert L. Akikta & Dr. Robert Lee Harris

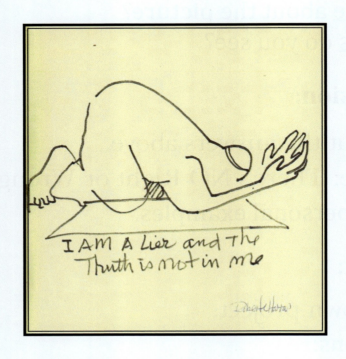

WHAT DOES THIS MEAN?

Questions & Answers:

1. How <u>do</u> you <u>see</u> the picture?
2. Do you <u>like</u> the picture?
3. Did you <u>care</u> about the picture?
4. What <u>colors</u> do you see?

Class Discussion:

- Talk about the answers above.
- Side Note: There's NO Right or Wrong Answers.
- Give life/personal examples.

Class Project:

Create your own project.
- Suggestions:
    A. Recreate and interpret your own version of the picture.
    B. Write your own commentary on the subject.
    C. Create a color schemes by using paints, crayons, clays and other substances for different textures.

Summary/Discussion:

1. Take away   2. What you learned?

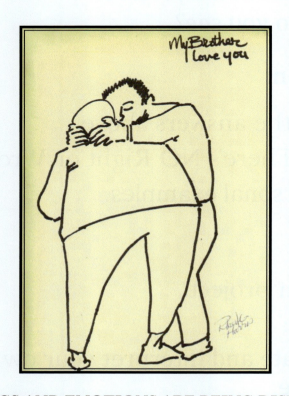

WHAT FEELINGS AND EMOTIONS ARE BEING DISPLAYED HERE?

Questions & Answers:

1. How <u>do</u> you <u>see</u> the picture?
2. Do you <u>like</u> the picture?
3. Did you <u>care</u> about the picture?
4. What <u>colors</u> do you see?

Class Discussion:

- Talk about the answers above.
- Side Note: There's NO Right or Wrong Answers.
- Give life/personal examples.

Class Project:

Create your own project.
- Suggestions:
    A. Journal your own commentary on the subject.
    B. Poste your thoughts
    C. Create your own unique images that illustrate love.
    D. Create color schemes by using paints, clays photos and using different textures.

Summary/Discussion:

1. Take away   2. What you learned?

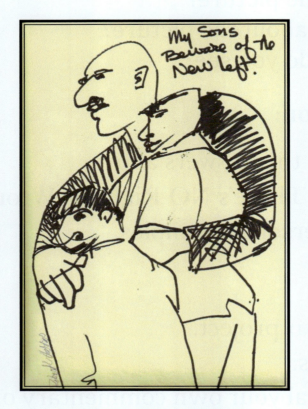

WHAT IS THE MESSAGE?

Questions & Answers:

1. How <u>do</u> you <u>see</u> the picture?
2. Do you <u>like</u> the picture?
3. Did you <u>care</u> about the picture?
4. What <u>colors</u> do you see?

Class Discussion:

- Talk about the answers above.
- Side Note: There's NO Right or Wrong Answers.
- Give life/personal examples.

Class Project:

Create your own project.
- Suggestions:
    A. Illustrate your message.
    B. Create a unique poem.
    C. Create different color schemes by using paints, cut paper etc.

Summary/Discussion:

1. Take away   2. What you learned?

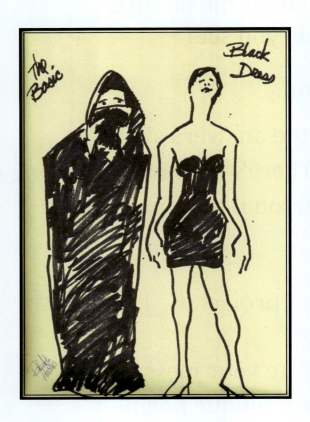

WHAT IS THIS COMENTING ON?

Questions & Answers:

1. How <u>do</u> you <u>see</u> the picture?
2. Do you <u>like</u> the picture?
3. Did you <u>care</u> about the picture?
4. What <u>colors</u> do you see?

Class Discussion:

- Talk about the answers above.
- Side Note: There's NO Right or Wrong Answers.
- Give life/personal examples.

Class Project:

Create your own project.
- Suggestions:
    A. Draw, paint, write or photograph your commentary on this subject.
    B. Create a YouTube video about this.
    C. Create stuffed dolls depicting or commenting on this theme.

Summary/Discussion:

1. Take away
2. What you learned?

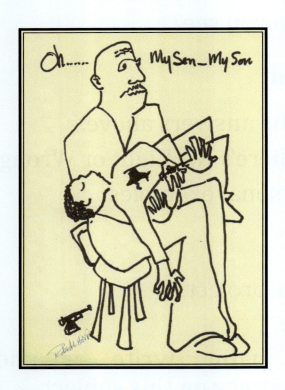

WHAT IS THIS IMAGE TELLING YOU?

Questions & Answers:

1. How <u>do</u> you <u>see</u> the picture?
2. Do you <u>like</u> the picture?
3. Did you <u>care</u> about the picture?
4. What <u>colors</u> do you see?

Class Discussion:

- Talk about the answers above.
- Side Note: There's NO Right or Wrong Answers.
- Give life/personal examples.

Class Project:

Create your own project.
- Suggestions:
  A. Journal, draw or verbally express your responses to this image.
  B. Create a unique response.
  C. Create and take some action.

Summary/Discussion:

1. Take away
2. What you learned?

About the Authors

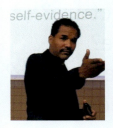

"See it before you believe it" is the mantra by which Dr. Robert L. Akikta lives. As the CEO and Founder of Power One Enterprises, LLC. Dr. Akikta prides himself on promoting both positive self-esteem and self-improvement. Robert was born and raised in Cincinnati, Ohio. Dr. Akikta is a graduate of both the University of Cincinnati and the University of Asian Martial Arts Studies, and a graduate from the School for the Creative and Performing Arts. Dr. Akikta is a certified martial arts educator and Hall of Fame inductee, and an ordained Elder from the New True Vine Based Ministries.

He provides martial arts educational services to adults and youth, in both school and group home settings across the nation, in the martial art called "Bushido" (the way of the warrior). It is a martial art that focuses on inner self-discipline. Dr. Akikta also uses the philosophy of martial arts science theories and methods to help youth/adult alike to become self-sufficient in mainstream society. The philosophy of martial arts science theories and methods is strongly interwoven in social emotional educational techniques, which demonstrates and illustrates how to help a person strengthen him or herself regardless of where they come from. In 2009 he received the "Master Instructor of the Year" award from the Indiana Karate Hall of Fame and is a certified Fatherhood and Healthy Relationship trainer. He is endorsed by Cincinnati City Council and recognized by many local community leaders. Dr. Akikta is well known among elite and average citizens, teachers, and students. In the faith based community he is acknowledged as a cornerstone of the community who helps shape the lives of all. Dr. Akikta is always seeking wisdom from God to do His will to engage, educate, and to empower others for the Kingdom of God. His dedication in serving people is a sight to behold: "See it before you believe it."

Dr. Robert Lee Harris was born in 1946 and contracted meningitis at the age of 8 months which left him permanently paralyzed in both legs and his left hand. He began championing the concept of ***inclusion*** at a young age. Fighting to continue his education after completing elementary classes at Condon School - which at the time was Cincinnati's only school for children with disabilities. He made his way into a somewhat accessible middle school and ultimately graduated from Central High School in 1965.

Since graduating from Gebhardt's Art School in 1968, Harris has become an accomplished artist with over 36 years of video production experience and over 50 years as a visual artist. Harris thinks of himself as a ***"Change Agent."*** His cable TV show is tiled: ***"Be the Change."*** The show is on 7 days a week and can be seen on Cincinnati's Government Access channel 23.

It is important to note that Harris's father was also an accomplished artist. His name was Raymond P. Harris and he was a graduate of the Cincinnati Art Academy. His image and work can be found in Life Magazine, July 13, 1953. The title of the article: "Turmoil Rules the Left Bank" on page 114.

January 16, 2006 Robert was presented the Lifetime Dream Keepers Award for his work. This was given to him by the Arts Consortium of Cincinnati.

In 2010 Harris was ordained as a pastor with the International Church for ALL Nations. There he serves as Pastor of Congregational Care. In 2013 he was inducted into the Ohio Civil Rights Hall of Fame. In 2015 he was awarded an honorary Doctorate of Divinity from Kingdom International Institute of Theology.

Currently Robert is one of the chess instructors for the Cris Collincworth Proscan Fund – teaching chess in Cincinnati's public schools. Robert has also been volunteering and presenting his program "Chess for Life." He has been working with youth who are housed at the Hamilton County Juvenile Court Center for over 12 years. His goal is to help them to understand that "Just because you can doesn't mean that you necessarily, should."

In the early half 2018 Harris completed his 3 year term as a board member for Hamilton county developmental disabilities services and began serving a 3 year term as a board member for the Southwest Ohio Regional Transit Authority (SORTA), an entity that operates a fixed-route bus service and paratransit for people with disabilities. Harris is also currently a chair on the board for the Cancer Justice Network.

Harris also serves on the board of the Center for Independent Living Options (CILO). This organization celebrated 40 years of service in 2017. Harris is one of its founders.

He is past president of the Board of Directors for the Cincinnati Human Relations Commission (CHRC).

The Greater Cincinnati Bicentennial Committee included Harris in its Portraits in ------' Excellence. Harris is an Ohio winner of the "Victory Award" which he received from former First Lady Barbara Bush at a ceremony at the White House. In 1994-he received the "Ohio Humanitarian Award - Employment Equality" from Governor George Voinovich. In 2002, Harris received the "Maurice McCracken Award for Peace and Justice" and in 2003 was included in Fifth Third Bank's "Profile in Courage." Harris' painting "Skyline" is part of the art collection of Cincinnati Bell.

In 2006, Harris was awarded the "Lifetime Dreamkeeper Award" from the Arts Consortium of Cincinnati and in August 2013, The Cincinnati METRO awarded Harris as a "Community Partner" for helping to make the transit system more accessible for those with disabilities. He is very active in the community and has been involved in many boards and committees, including the Ohio Arts Council's Artist with Disabilities Advisory Council, the Contemporary Art Center, the United Cerebral Palsy Center, University Affiliated Center for Developmental Disorders, the Aronoff Center, the American Red Cross, Housing Opportunities Made Equal, United Way and Community Chest. He served as a member of the Community Advisory Committee of the National Underground Railroad Freedom Center. Also, he served as the Disability Advisor.

He has served as an Inclusion Consultant for the Cinergy Children's Museum of Cincinnati and the Cincinnati Reds Architectural Design Team, and others. He has also provided services for the Greater Cincinnati Region of the National Conference for Community and Justice [now known as "BRIDGES for a Just Community] and as a Marketing Representative for the Ohio Rehabilitation Services Commission in the Cincinnati/Dayton area.

Editor

Dr. Steve C. Sunderland is a peace activist, creating organizations, works of art, and relationships that promote peace. Now, Director of the Cancer Justice Network, a branch of the Peace Village, this work flows out of a concern that injustice in health is causing friction, conflict, death, and war. Steve has been a professor of peace and a dean at the University of Cincinnati for 35 years, dean of the College for Human Services, for 9 years, and a staff member at Antioch College, National Training Laboratories, National Student Association, and a continuing member of the Civil Rights Movement. Along the way, I have co-founded Fernside: Cincinnati Center for Grieving Children; Parents of Murdered Children, Survivors After Suicide, and Parents of Stigmatized Death. Steve is married, has 7 children, 12 grandchildren, and a hot banjo.

Printed in the United States
By Bookmasters